A LITTLE CATECHISM
ON THE HOLY ROSARY

A LITTLE CATECHISM
ON THE HOLY ROSARY

IN RELATION TO THE IMAGE OF
OUR LADY OF GUADALUPE

by Miguel Guadalupe

PUBLISHING COMPANY
P.O Box 42028 Santa Barbara, CA 93140-2028
(800) 647-9882 • (805) 957-4893 • Fax: (805) 957-1631

Library of Congress #: 96-07084

Published by:
Queenship Publishing
P.O. Box 42028
Santa Barbara, CA 93140-2028
(800) 647-9882 • (805) 957-4893 • Fax: (805) 957-1631

Printed in the United States of America

ISBN: 1-882972-78-3

CONTENTS

INTRODUCTION

Although the Rosary is a very simple prayer, it reveals unexpected dimensions for those who enter more
deeply into it through meditation. When properly prayed,
it even helps us to better understand why Our Lady in-
sistently pleads for its recitation.[1] Little by little, we may
even be granted the grace to understand something of
its apocalyptic significance.

We are nearing the completion of this second
millenium with very little, if any, consideration or pre-
occupation at all about "how" or "when" the "end times"
will be. In any secular or personal activity, especially as
it nears its close, we find ourselves, almost instinctively,

---

[1] Our Lady gave the Rosary to St. Dominic as heaven's assistance
in the fight against heresies. A Rosary Crusade saved Christendom
from the invasion of the Turks at the Battle of Lepanto, 1571. At
Lourdes, Our Lady prayed the Rosary with St. Bernadette. At
Fatima, Our Lady presented herself as "the Lady of the Rosary"
and told Francisco that he was to pray many Rosaries. She asked
the children to pray the Rosary everyday in honor of Our Lady of
the Rosary. Our Lady has even made many promises to any and
all who pray the Holy Rosary. Throughout the history of the
Church great heroes and heroines of GOD and Our Lady alike
have risen up to defend and promote true devotion to Our Lady
and to the Holy Rosary.

assessing our "part" in it. These natural level assessments can serve as a means of preparation for that final account to be given at the end of our earthly life. It is GOD's mercy, through MARY, that the Holy Rosary has been given to man, for in its containing all the mysteries of Salvation, it is our best help in preparing us for "that account" that is of eternal consequence. Our life, along with the life of every other human being, must be resumed in the mysteries of Salvation of the Rosary, and it is thus, more than any other prayer, that the Rosary reveals itself to be a "PRAYER OF HARVEST."

Giving an account means that we have to think over things more profoundly. We have to learn to become meditative, pondering over things in our hearts as Our Lady did on every word and deed of her SON. When prayed with one's whole heart, the Rosary becomes the simplest and best help for meditation. In her constant plea for her children to pray the Rosary, Our Lady seems to promise that it will unlock the mysteries of the Reign of Heaven for those who faithfully pray it.

True meditation aims at incarnating that which is meditated, such that little by little, one's meditation reflects more perfectly the life of order of the Reign of GOD. This order of the Reign of GOD is not only materially indicated by the mysteries of the Rosary, but also

---

[2] The formal structure of the Rosary is its formal order, i.e., the prayers of the Rosary each have a form and those prayers are prayed in a certain numerical manner, i.e., we pray: the Apostle's Creed once, one Our Father, three Hail Mary's, one Glory be...,

by its structure.[2] As much as the Gospel of St. John helps in its formal structure to understand the Trinitarian perspective of the Life of JESUS, so will the formal meditation of the Rosary help us to understand that the Rosary indeed is a Trinitarian prayer and so instantly reminds us that our faith is in THE TRIUNE GOD: in THE FATHER, THE SON and THE HOLY SPIRIT.[3]

The Holy Rosary is a prayer of great transparence, so much so that both its exterior form and material composition have deep symbolic significances. The cross and the beads, for example, should both be of wood, such that when we pray, we can consciously take in all of material creation into our prayer. This is also the deeper significance of the wood of the Cross on which Our LORD JESUS CHRIST died. It represents creation in its four directions.

The interior contemplation of the mysteries of Salvation as we pronounce the words of the Rosary should be a means of sanctifying all of our spoken words, because the word is the means by which we express ourselves. It is through the "word" that we are related to the WORD, the Second Divine Person. This is also why we have to give an account for every one of our words. The

---

[2 cont.] announce a mystery, one Our Father, ten Hail Mary's, one Glory be..., one "Oh my JESUS," etc.,.. it is "poetry from heaven" and so not only the contents (= the mysteries), but also the form in which they are presented are part of its "message."

[3] (not only in JESUS as man, or in the HOLY SPIRIT as some kind of "spirit")

Rosary teaches us to think before we speak. It helps us to respond more justly to the dignity of being related to the THE WORD OF GOD.

The word alone is not sufficient. The Rosary loses all its spiritual dimension if only the formula of words are used in an automatic recitation. The formal structure of the Rosary can only be brought to its consummation when we meditate the mysteries of Salvation in the HOLY SPIRIT and thus approach contemplation: seeing before our interior eyes what we meditate!

As the Rosary is a Trintiarian prayer, it will guard us against simplifications as well as all other variations of heresies linked to the Person of JESUS. Looking to the image of Our Lady of Guadalupe while we pray the Rosary, is an important help to contemplation. With and through MARY, we will be able to recognize Our LORD before us as HE IS IN THE SPIRIT and thus will we realize the Rosary to be our true guard against the snares of any anti-christ who tries to present himself as the "messiah."

Contemplation is the best means to approach THE

---

4   Let us recall the four transcendentals of metaphysics: "Unum, Verum, Bonum, Pulchrum" (Unity, Truth, Good, Beauty) - Beauty is the consummation of the first three! The cathedrals of the Medieval Age are an reflection of the beauty of revelation, but when we contemplate the Beauty of Revelation present in the image of Guadalupe we find the "masterpiece of the Divine Artist."

BEAUTY OF REVELATION.[4] The formal meditation of the Rosary, together with the image of Our Lady of Guadalupe, helps us to find our way back to the BEAUTY OF GOD. GOD Himself reveals MARY to be His Masterpiece, reflection of HIS INVISIBLE BEAUTY in and through the Rosary and the image HE Himself made. Contemplating the Beauty of GOD helps to transform our poorly recited Rosary into a prayer of praise, adoration and gratitude for the immeasurable grace of Redemption. Contemplating the Beauty of GOD enables us to live our consecration to MARY more consciously. In this Beauty, the contemplation of the Rosary becomes an indispensable weapon and prayer of defense in the hand and heart of any child or servant of MARY. Should we not *"shine like the stars amidst a corrupted generation?"*[5]

We need to trust in the power of the mysteries of Salvation! In the same manner that we beseech to be covered with the protective mantle of MARY sheltering the LIFE of her BELOVED SON, so are we to beseech that others be covered by the mysteries of Salvation. In this way, the Rosary not only is a means of interceding on behalf of all those who have gone astray,

---

[5]   PHIL 2:15: Here again the importance of LIGHT as the distinction of a Christian is emphasized. The more we unite with the angels, we will become "children of light" (cf. 1 THES. 5:5) as they are "light of the LIGHT OF GOD!"

but by way of the mysteries it becomes a prayer of reparation.....especially when we conclude the mysteries with the reparation prayer given by Our Lady at Fatima.[6]

We should consciously invite our guardian angel, the guardian angels of all those entrusted to our care and St. Gabriel, he who first addressed Our Lady with the salutation: *"Ave, Gratia Plena,"* to pray this great prayer of Beauty, Order and Love with us.[7]

---

[6]   "Oh my JESUS, forgive us our sins. Save us from the fire of hell. Lead all souls to heaven, and help all those in most need of your mercy."

[7]   The Jerusalem Bible tells us that St. Luke wrote his Gospel in Greek, and that the "Ave" of St. Gabriel translates to the Hebrew "Shalom": Peace. This first word of St. Gabriel to the Blessed Virgin corresponds beautifully with the word of the Angel of Portugal in his first apparition to the three shepherd children: "Do not be afraid! I am the Angel of Peace...." The word "peace," along with who the Blessed Virgin revealed herself to be, "I am the Lady of the Rosary," in a certain way hint to us of this great Archangel's assistance in praying the Rosary (a prayer with formal elements of more than 150 Ave Maria's) as well as his mission with respect to the Incarnation of the SON of the Most HIGH in our hearts minds and souls.

I

WHAT IS THE SIGNIFICANCE OF THE EXTERIOR ROSARY?[8]

1. Why is the Cross found at the beginning of the Rosary?

The Cross is a sign of Our LORD JESUS CHRIST in, with and through Whom we are redeemed.

All mysteries of the Life, Death and Resurrection of CHRIST encircle this definitive sign of Salvation. Not only is it found in the Sorrowful Mysteries, but also

---

[8] To show the relationship of the Holy Rosary to the image of Our Lady of Guadalupe, we must reflect on the significance and the structure of the Rosary which, as we will later see, parallels that of the image of Guadalupe.

in the Joyful and Glorious. The SON of GOD encounters the Cross already at the Incarnation and only by way of the Cross does Creation come to its consummation in the Glorious Mysteries.

In praying the Holy Rosary, the Cross can be likened unto the "key" which opens the door of the mysteries held therein. The mysteries of the Holy Rosary will truly incarnate in us when we are crucified with CHRIST.

2. What is the significance of the beads of the Rosary?

The Rosary is the unfolding of the mystery of the Cross. This is why there should be little crosses instead of round beads. It is the faithful love of Our Lady that has taken all the mysteries of the "cross" into her Heart, making all the rough edges of the "crosses" round by her continual contemplation.

3. Why we say "Rose" - ary?

Having become rounded, the mysteries of the Rosary exhale the "sweet smelling perfume of the Gospel"[9] and blossom forth revealing the deeper beauty of Salvation. Just as the entire construction of the Rosary is Trinitarian, so also are its individual elements. In a deeper sense, each bead can be likened unto a drop of the Most Precious Blood of Our LORD JESUS CHRIST. Collectively, these drops of Blood reflect the Love of GOD, and His desire to make each member of the Mystical Body of CHRIST into a beautiful rose for the greater praise of the TRIUNE GOD. In this transparent way, the beads of the Rosary also represent each member of the Church, for every soul belonging to the Mystical Body of CHRIST has a special and unique relation to one of the mysteries of Salvation. The special sign of revelation through MARY is that the mysteries of Salvation reveal their deepest beauty. It is not a coincidence that GOD the FATHER, by way of the Virgin MARY and Blessed Juan Diego, sent roses to the Bishop as a proof of the authenticity of the revelation.[10]

---

[9] cf. II COR 2:15
[10] cf. Nican Mopohua, vs. 125-183

They are exceptional roses, grown up in cold Winter and on a stony soil[11] and therefore a profound sign with multiple dimensions:

• They point to the mysteries of Salvation in CHRIST which should unfold in the hearts of the faithful when the Gospel is proclaimed.

• They reflect the Most Precious Blood flowing forth from the Wounds of Our LORD JESUS CHRIST to save us and make us one in His Mystical Body, the Church. Therefore, every bead

---

[11] Verse three of the Nican Mopohua tells us that the marvel of Guadalupe began in the first days of December, and verses 129, 132 and 133 that it would have been naturally impossible to find roses where only ice, weeds, thorns, cactus and mesquites are prevalent.

prayed in love becomes like a drop of His Most Precious Blood.[12]

- They are also a sign of the souls which have ripened in the cold winter of a pagan domination and are now ready for the harvest, because Our Lady of Guadalupe appearing in 1531 is really and truly the MOTHER OF HARVEST.[13]

4. Why does the Rosary begin with five beads? (1 + 3 + 1)

This is the first external indication that the Five Wounds of Our LORD are mysteriously present in the

---

[12] In the Aztec culture, man was considered *"macehualli"* - he who merits participation in Divine Life only through penance and suffering. Man's only hope of even approaching GOD other than sacrificial death was through beauty: flower and song. It is for this reason that flowers were almost looked upon as the "the embodiment of GOD of earth," and the roses as the "sign" of authenticity - the medium used by heaven for the "great sign" left on the tilma of Juan Diego - are somewhat of an "embodiment of GOD on earth," of the incarnation of the "most precious" that heaven and earth can offer.

[13] Within seven short years after the appearance of the Virgin on Tepeyac, eight million Aztecs were baptized. It is almost a tripling in number of the three million who left the Church in Europe at the onset of the Protestant Reformation. The harvesting Our Lady began in 1531 continues on to this day. In and through her miraculous image, she has become the most visited person in the world. She receives more visitors annually than St. Peter's in Rome.

Rosary. The Wounds of Our LORD free man from the captivity of the five-pointed star which the devil wants to put over his limbs, senses and faculties.[14]

The first bead reminds us that all our prayer, with MARY, through the SON, is directed to the FATHER.

But it will reach HIM only if we pray in the force of the Three Theological Virtues of **Faith**, **Hope** and **Love**. (2nd - 4th bead)

Our prayer, as in everything we do, should be to the greater glory of the Triune GOD. (5th bead)

---

[14] The four main faculties of man: will, sentiment, intelligence and senses, are meant to help him orient his life to GOD. They are symbolized in the four directions of the wind, because their ultimate aim is to come to know GOD. As such, they are bundled together, they are related to each other and they compliment each other. Just as the Four Gospels are one in JESUS CHRIST, so also should the four faculties become one in man's center, in his heart. Man's balance is broken whenever a particular faculty is singled out at the exclusion of the others. Modern philosophy, with its innumerable "isms," provides a vivid example of this disequilibrium. When man makes "will" his only orientation, he becomes a dictator; when he exclusively lives his sentiments, he becomes a romantic; when he governs his life strictly by his intelligence, he becomes a cold rationalist; and when he follows only his senses, he is lost to this earth.

5. Why are there three Rosaries?

Our LORD JESUS CHRIST always represents the Triune GOD, and as the mysteries of the Rosary are Christo-centric, so also will they necessarily reflect the Most Holy TRINITY. This reflection of the Triune GOD is first of all recognized in the three important stages of Our LORD's Life: His Incarnation, His Passion and His Resurrection. In the Incarnation, JESUS is the FATHER's gift to us poor sinners. He invites us to enter into His Life and so become sons in the SON.

In the Passion, it is the SON of GOD Who first of all captures our attention. By way of His Five Wounds, He frees us from the prison of sin.

In the mysteries of the Resurrection, we see the work of the HOLY SPIRIT, sent by the FATHER to consummate Redemption.

6. Why does the Rosary form a ring (a crown)?

The ring is a symbol of GOD's Life; HE is all perfect in Himself. In GOD there is the fullness of eternal beatitude.[15] By way of the Cross of the SON we are called to enter in this deeper Life of GOD, and through prayer it will be realized in us.[16]

All mysteries are in GOD. The more we enter into them by meditation, the more we participate in Divine Life. The circle of the mysteries must become, for us earthly pilgrims, a spiral which will lift us up ever closer to GOD from the heaviness of this earth and the burden of sin. This is why we cannot just repeat the mysteries over and over again, we must enter into them and through them finally become a living mystery of GOD.[17]

---

[15] This mystery is reflected in the halo of the angels and Saints. It is an indication that their life rests in GOD and has found its consummation in GOD.

[16] Here, we begin to see that the movement of living prayer is circular. Little by little, our prayer should enter into the circular movement of Divine Life. The spiral movement can be best seen in the Gospel of St. John. See the Eucharistic Sermon of Our LORD in the sixth chapter of the Gospel of St. John.

[17] This is the last finality of the liturgy of the Church in all its "repetition." For the faithful, true liturgy is never repetition. It is a living spiral that lifts us up to the Heart of GOD.

Our faithful guardian angel is the help of the HOLY SPIRIT given to us to discover the mystery of Salvation which has an existential relation to us. If only we persevere in praying the Rosary, we will soon find that mystery among the fifteen to which our life is co-ordinated in a special way. If we pray the Rosary in the living circle of the spiral as MARY did, it will become for us the crown of victory which we will wear for the greater glory and honor of GOD for all eternity, and this crown will be part of hers.

II

WHAT IS THE STRUCTURE OF THE ROSARY AS THE INTERIOR HOUSE?

1. In what sense is the Rosary a "house"?

a. The mysteries of Salvation in CHRIST, as an integral make-up of the liturgical year of the Church, are the fundamental structure of the house of GOD on this earth orientated to the New Jerusalem for its consummation. Our meditation of the mysteries of Salvation allow the House of GOD to grow in us, in JESUS CHRIST. Architect and constructor of this House is the HOLY SPIRIT, masons are the Holy Angels.

b. MARY, with her unconditional "Yes" to GOD, is the cornerstone of the House of GOD. Out of her transpierced heart rise the Four Columns, another symbol for the Cross.[18] It is in this house that the Triune GOD wills to dwell with us.

---

[18] The Four Columns of the House of GOD reflect the four major attributes of GOD: His Holiness, His Wisdom, His Justice and His Omnipotence.

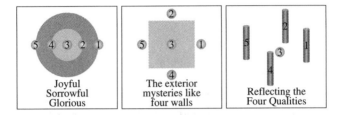

Joyful Sorrowful Glorious	The exterior mysteries like four walls	Reflecting the Four Qualities

c. A symbol for this indwelling of the TRIUNE GOD in the Rosary are the 3 X 4 mysteries (three rosaries each with four exterior mysteries) including the central mystery. The four exterior mysteries of each rosary (Joyful, Sorrowful and Glorious) become like four walls surrounding its respective central mystery. They reflect the description of Eden surrounded by the four rivers.[19]

d. The central mysteries of the three Rosaries: the Nativity, the Crowning with Thorns and the Descent of the HOLY SPIRIT, are a symbol for "the triple Birth of the LORD in the soul of the faithful. (cf. II.2.a.)

---

[19] Cf. GEN. 2:10-14

2. How is the TRIUNE GOD coming to birth in the soul through the Rosary?

a. The "Birth" of JESUS is indicated in the three central mysteries:

In the Joyful Mysteries, it is a birth in joy; it is the joy any soul experiences at the onset of its spiritual life.

It is a birth in pain in the mystery of the Crowning with Thorns, for only through thorns of scorn, being held in contempt and rejected can we truly imitate Our Thorn-Crowned LORD and come to share in His Royal Priesthood.

Joyful   Sorrowful   Glorious

It is a birth in glory by the Descent of the HOLY SPIRIT upon the Apostles on the Feast of Pentecost.

But these three "births," in view of the TRIUNE GOD, are really one. They are one as GOD in THREE IS ONE.

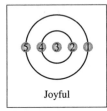

Joyful

Sorrowful

Glorious

b.   The 3 X 3 circles as "a way of birth"

The four exterior mysteries of each Rosary can easily be recognized as two circles about a central mystery.(The 1st and 5th mysteries form a circle and the 2nd and 4th mysteries form another circle.)[20]

As part of the spiral of the Rosary the central mystery is found to be the most interior "circle" of

---

[20]   Just as Our LORD JESUS employed parables to explain the mysteries of the Kingdom of GOD to His disciples, so also do we employ the use of an "interior structure" to help our poor understanding with respect to the same mysteries. Geometry proposes the question: "How does a quadrangle become a circle?" This may seem like an abstract logic of contradiction, but considering the laws of the quadrangle and the circle together help us to enter deeper into the mysteries of our faith. The Triune GOD (Three in one), by way of the Incarnation of the WORD, in a mysterious way becomes "Four." In this way, the bridge between three and four is made. GOD Who is Three, in a mysterious way, is inhoused {contained, inherent, composed} in "four," but remains dwelling in it as "Three" at the same time.

each rosary. In this perspective each Rosary is made up of three circles, and being that there are three Rosaries we have a final product of nine circles.[21]

These nine circles indicate that the birth of GOD in the soul, through MARY, has nine steps.[22]

c. The motor behind the circles is opposition

1. There is an opposition between the mysteries coordinated to the circles.
   a. In the Joyful Mysteries
      - In the first exterior circle: + The Annuciation and * The Loss of JESUS in Jerusalem, the opposition is that of receiving and losing (and finding again).
      - In the second exterior circle: + The Visitation and the * Presentation, it is the opposition between the first two Commandments – Love of GOD and love of neighbor.

---

[21] "The ring of light of GOD," previously mentioned as being the halos of the Angels and Saints, is that sign of a perfect and mysterious union with GOD. We not only consider the central mystery of each Rosary as being a separate circle surrounded by two other exterior circles, but we must first of all recognize that the spiral movement of the two exterior circles tends toward the interior circle. The Birth of GOD in man, tends to the deepest recess of his soul.

[22] "Nine" months is the normal term in the formation of a child in the womb of its mother before its natural birth.

    b. In the Sorrowful Mysteries
- In the first exterior circle: + the Agony and * The Crucifixion, it is the opposition of interior combat and exterior confession.
- In the second exterior circle: + The Flagellation and * The Carrying of the Cross, it is the opposition of static and dynamic perseverance.

 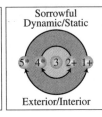 

    c. In the Glorious Mysteries
- In the first exterior circle: + The Resurrrection and * The Crowning of MARY in Heaven, it is the opposition of opening and consummating the way to Heaven.
- In the second exterior circle: + The Ascension and * The Assumption, it is the opposition of the LORD's going home and taking up to Him the material creation.

2. There is also an opposition between the exterior rings (between the circle of the 1st and 5th Mysteries with the circle of the 2nd and 4th Mysteries):

   a. With the Joyful Mysteries, the opposition between the exterior ring of the Annunciation and the Finding in the Temple with the ring of the Visitation and the Presention, is one of **Receiving and Giving**.

   b. With the Sorrowful Mysteries, the opposition between the exterior ring of the Agony and the Crucifixion with the ring of the Flagellation and the Carrying of the Cross, is one of **goal and way**.

   c. With the Glorious Mysteries, the opposition between the exterior ring of the Resurrection and the Crowning of MARY, with the exterior ring of the Ascension and the Assumption, is that the **way to heaven is opened and the force of the gravity of the earth overcome**.

      The common denominator of all opposition in the Holy Rosary is the opposition of the vertical and the horizontal. The Cross that initiates the Holy Rosary, is giving its last fruit of consummation (already announced at the end of the first Genesis account of Creation).Cf. GEN 2:1-4

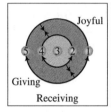  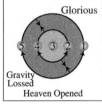

3. The Resolution of Opposition is found in the Central Mysteries of each Rosary. It is the Promise of Transformation which will even begin on earth if we submit to the trial of the Cross.

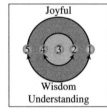  

3. How does the Life of CHRIST develop in us in the HOLY SPIRIT?

a. We can consider the 3 X 2 circles and the one circle in the middle[23] as an image of all spiritual growth towards JESUS.

---

[23] The three central mysteries form the one mystery of the triple Birth of Our LORD in our souls and therefore also, they form the one interior circle. The structure of the Rosary as 3 x 2 circles thus becomes (3 x 2) + 1.

b. The 3 X 2 exterior circles are like six steps towards consummation if we look at them in the light of the Seven Gifts of the HOLY SPIRIT. The exterior circle formed by the mysteries of the The Annunciation and Loss of JESUS in Jerusalem (in the oppostion of receiving and giving) corresponds to the **Gift of Understanding**. We need this gift of Understanding throughout the journey of our earthly pilgrimage. We will enjoy the fullness of Understanding only in the beatific vision.

   The exterior circle formed by the mysteries of The Visitation and The Presentation in the Temple (in the opposition of the two Great Commandments) is our second step towards consummation. Correlated with the **Gift of Wisdom** we learn that the criterium of a genuine love of GOD is our love of neighbor.

   The third step results from the circle formed by the mysteries of The Agony in the Garden and The Crucifixion. The **Gift of Counsel** reminds us that we will not be able to be confessors (external confession) if we have not yet overcome our own will (internal combat). We must be completely conformed and accommodated to the Will of GOD.

   The **Gift of Fortitude** corresponds with the circle formed by the mysteries of The Flagellation and The Carrying the Cross (in the opposition of static and dynamic perserverance). This fourth step enables us to combat the tempatations and attacks of the devil.

The fifth step is formed by the circle of The Resurrection and the Crowning of MARY. The opposition of opening and consummating the way to heaven reflected by these mysteries corresponds to the

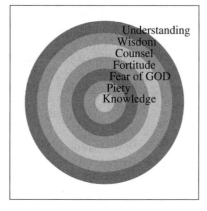

Gift of the Fear of GOD, for only GOD can help us to break the prison of sin.

The Ascension and the Assumption, in the opposition of the LORD's going home and taking up to Him the material creation, correspond to the **Gift of Piety**. Like the LORD on the Cross, we must overcome. Only then can we more fully partake in the beatitude of heaven.

These six steps are like circles around the central mystery of the triple Birth of Our LORD. This last step corresponds to the **Gift of Knowledge.** The fullness of the Birth of CHRIST in our hearts is the most important science we ought to acquire in life.[24]

---

[24]   Our active part is to get rid of the obstacles and surrender our good will to the greater Will of GOD, the rest is left to GOD: we only have to "suffer" being transformed according to HIS IMAGE!

4. How can we participate deeper in the mysteries of the Rosary?

a. Our "yes" to **love MARY**, in union with our Holy Angel in ADORATION, becomes a "yes" to love the Triune GOD.

b. **Serving MARY** and GOD through her, requires CONTEMPLATION and REPARATION on our part.

c. **Walking with MARY** is our MISSION of participation in the consummation of creation.

III

WHAT RELATION DOES THE ROSARY HAVE WITH THE CONTEMPLATION OF THE IMAGE OF OUR LADY OF GUADALUPE?

A – A RELATION OF EXTERIOR FORM[25]

1. The Cross at the beginning of the Rosary

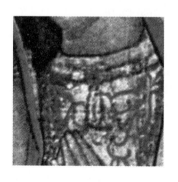

The little cross on the golden brooch at the neckline of Our Lady's gown perfectly corresponds with the cross that we take up when we begin to pray the Rosary. Salvation is wide and reaches out to all cre-

---

[25] cf. I. 1. - 6, pgs. 4-9

ation, but like the little cross, the door of entry is "narrow."[26]

We can easily imagine that the Rosary hanging on the cross, embraces the entire figure of Our Lady. It follows the movement of ransom which starts in her eyes. By way of meditation of the mysteries of the Life, Death and Resurrection of her SON, she wants to bring home all those who follow the attraction of the Love of GOD.

2. The significance of the beads of the Rosary

We recall that only by the constant meditation of the mysteries of the Life of her SON have the cross beads become rounded. This tranformation of the rough edges

---

[26] Under the golden brooch with the small cross we note that the white ermine lining of Our Lady's gown is brought together. This bringing together of a larger neckline has many layers of interpretation. First of all, the gown of Our Lady symbolizes all of salvation history. The white ermine lining tells us that this history comes to its fullness in MARY (cf. GAL 4:4); the fullness of time is brought together in the form of the Hebrew "Tau" - cross, and upon this "white gathering" is found THE CROSS of CHRIST. Being that all this silent gospel takes place at the neckline of Our Lady helps us to understand something of MARY's role in the Mystical Body of her SON and her mission as the Mediatrix of all grace.

of the cross to smooth ones is contemplated in the four-petalled flower on Our Lady's womb.[27] The small, almost insignificant flower, is a symbol of the SON of GOD, the SON of MARY, Who has saved us by His suffering on the Cross.

In the SON, the Cross is like a sword the FATHER sends to the earth to consummate the separation of darkness and light. Already at the Annunciation of the Incarnation, MARY surrendered completely to this sword of the FATHER. Day and night she meditated its significance and it was thus that her praying of this mystery has made it round and joyful for us.

The little four-petalled flower is not only an image of the sharp Cross of the FATHER made round, it is also the sign of the LAMB of GOD. Its rounded form exemplifies Our LORD's humility: "He was led like a lamb to the slaughter, ... opening not his mouth."[28] This sign embraces the Four Cardinal Directions of the Wind, the four basic elements and the four facul-

---

[27] The four-petalled flower superimposed on the womb of Our Lady is a symbol form found in all of the ancient cultures of the world. It is a symbol reserved for GOD. Among the Aztecs and Nahua-Toltecan people this four-petalled flower, better known as *"Nahui Ollin,"* has more than eighty significant features, all of which speak or reverberate the divine attributes. The fact that the flower is over the womb of this woman who wears a sash (the sash notifying all beholders of pregnancy) tells that she is *TEOTOKOS*, bearer of GOD.

[28] ISAIAH 53:7

ties of man which, by the Cross, will receive their ultimate perfection.[29]

3. "Rose" - ary

Bishop Juan Zumarraga could not believe in the authenticity of the Virgin's request based on the mere verbal testimony of Juan Diego.[30] This is why Our Lady responded to his hidden petition by giving the "sign" of the Castilian roses. Symbolically, this hierarchical petition of the Church's interior longing for the arrival of the "great sign" is fullfilled by means of the roses in 1531.[31] Heaven not only responds to the secret plea of the hierarchical Church, but also opens our eyes of faith for the "woman all in white, brighter than the sun..." who on May 13, 1917, called herself the "Lady of the Rosary."[32]

The use of this title, together with the chosen instrumentation of three shepherd children, is heaven's way of again placing the mysteries of salvation as "roses" at the feet of the hierarchical Church.

---

[29] cf. footnote #14, MATT 24:31 and MK. 13:27

[30] cf. Nican Mopohua, vs.78 and 80

[31] Those secretly petitioned by Bishop Juan Zumarraga, those found, cut and gathered by Blessed Juan Diego, the same rearranged by the Virgin as "the sign" and used by heaven as the medium for the miraculous imprinting of the Virgin on the tilma of Juan Diego.

[32] cf. Memorias da Irma Lucia, 2nd Edition, 1977

The triple testimony at Fatima accentuates the triple significance of the boy at the feet of Our Lady of Guadalupe as **messenger of the Most Holy TRINITY**.[33] Filled with zeal on behalf of the conversion of sinners, Lucia, Francisco and Jacinta surrender themselves totally to GOD in and through the mission they receive from the Angel and from Our Lady. Like the roses given to Juan Diego, slowly unfolding as "the sign" of authenticity, the three shepherd children of Fatima are a triple testimony of unity for the entire Church.

In relation to the FATHER, the three children are called to give witness by their lives. By their word, they give witness on behalf of the SON and in their union they give witness in the HOLY SPIRIT. In the image of Our Lady of Guadalupe this triple witness is symbolized in the three colors of the wings: blue for water, red for blood and white for the HOLY SPIRIT.[34]

In the tilma of Juan Diego, the union of roses and image tell us that MARY is THE MYSTICAL ROSE

---

[33] The triple significance of the boy at the feet of the Virgin of Guadalupe is: to the FATHER - child, to the SON - victim and to the HOLY SPIRIT - angel.

[34] cf. IJN 5:6-8; Red, as a symbol of fire, is usually the color attributed to the HOLY SPIRIT. Here, it is white to remind us that in the end, the entire Church must be in perfect union with the Holy Angels, instruments of the HOLY SPIRIT for the consummation of all things, as exposed in the Apocalypse. Only purified by the fire of persecution will the Church be able to reflect the purity of the Immaculate Heart of MARY.

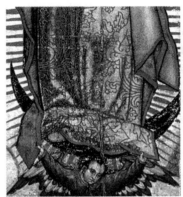

OF GOD.[35] In MARY and through MARY the mysteries of JESUS CHRIST exude their wonderful perfume.

The Rosary is A GIFT OF THE LOVE OF GOD to Christendom by means of which the HOLY SPIRIT wants to enkindle the interior life of grace.[36] More and

---

[35] "Mystical Rose" is one of the advocations of the Blessed Virgin MARY sung by the Church for centuries. cf. Litany of Loretto.

[36] Remember that it was first necessary to lay the foundation, to build the walls of the House of GOD. This was the static mission of the Benedictine Monks. The Mendicant Orders, Franciscans and Dominicans, were the first to carry the Good News to people; only with St. Ignatius and the Jesuits the HOLY SPIRIT pointed towards the importance of individual conversion. The Rosary comprises these three perspectives:
  - as "interior house,"
  - by the "movements" of the mysteries,
  - finally with their call to incarnate them in our life!

more, the blossoming of the mysteries of the Life, Suffering and Resurrection of CHRIST will fill the Church with the sweet aroma of Salvation.

The apparition of Our Lady of Guadalupe in 1531, the beginning of Modern Times, as the "Woman clothed with the sun," should be a reminder to the Church that: only in the power of the beauty of MARY will we find the means to overcome the forces of hell.[37]

Through the image of the rose, GOD wants to reveal Himself, not only as *UNUM, VERUM, and BONUM*,[38] but HE also wants to reveal His beauty by way of her who so perfectly reflects His Beauty: *"Tota Pulchra"* in whom not even the smallest trace of sin is to be found. This is why she was worthy to be as *Teotokos* the Mother of the BEAUTIFUL LOVE. This maternity

---

[37] Pope John Paul II entrusted his papacy to the Virgin of Guadalupe during his first pastoral visit to Mexico, under her title "HELP OF ALL CHRISTIANS." Church history has it written that this advocation of Our Blessed Mother, along with the title "Queen of the Rosary," were given to her by Pope Pius V after Christendom's victory over the Turks at the Battle of Lepanto (October 7, 1571) where a copy image of the Virgin of Guadalupe was of great importance to the united forces of the Spanish Armada and Venetian fleets. These apparently insignificant details are beautiful transparencies in which we recognize the Providence of Our Loving GOD.

[38] Remember: classical philosophy speaks of three "transcendental" properties of all existence: *UNUM, VERUM, BONUM* - UNITY, TRUTH, and EXCELLENCE.

of the Beautiful Love is symbolized in the dark red roses, reflecting the beauty of the Precious Blood and the Sacred Wounds of Our LORD JESUS CHRIST. As part of the "Folly of the Cross," it is a beauty that is only understood by those who love GOD.

More and more, in and through MARY, the HOLY SPIRIT will reveal interior depths of the mysteries of salvation which are synthesized in the Rosary. In and through MARY HE will open the interior space of our souls.[39]

The celestial beauty of the image of Guadalupe also reveals the beauty of the souls of all those who have grown in the middle of the Church out of the Wounds, the Precious Blood and the Sacred Heart of Our LORD. The nine large flowers, seeming to be inverted hearts pointing upwards, are another symbol for this growth in the Love of GOD.

4. The significance of the first five beads in relation to the image

The image of Our Lady of Guadalupe is that of the "GLORIOUS WOMAN." As such, we must seek out

---

[39] This "opening of interior spaces of the soul" is greatly noted at the beginning of the second Millennium with the German "Mystics of Light": Eckehart, Tauler, Seuse, St. Gertrude of Helfta and other mystical Saints. It is with them that devotion to the Sacred Heart of Our LORD began.

the mystery of the Wounds of Our LORD in their trans-figuration. Symbolically, we find this power of the victory of the LORD on the Cross in the cruciform figure of Our Lady.[40] By way of the Cross, man is called to grow into the holy order of the Reign of GOD.

Faith, Hope and Love also are the condition for our entering deeper into contemplation. This is symbolically portrayed in the first three large golden flowers super-imposed on Our Lady's chest. They are like one.

In the image, they are also a symbol of the inhabitation of the Triune GOD in the Heart of MARY Immaculate. All the graces she mediates necessarily spring forth from this mystery of the presence of the TRIUNE GOD in her Heart. (2nd - 4th bead)

As in the Rosary, all our prayer and contemplation should be orientated to the greater Glory of GOD. In the beauty of the image of Guadalupe, this truth is reflected in the fullness of light which falls upon her blessed womb.

---

[40] The cruciform figure of Our Lady is seen in the crossing of the vertical (the second column) with the horizontal (hands and arms united in prayer). The Cross is not an outward sign with her (as we do when we put up a cross in our rooms), but an interior reality. The little cross of her brooch is the only exterior sign of the cross we can find in the image. Like Our Lady, man also has to become cruciform. This is beautifully imaged for us in the messenger with outstretched arms at her feet.

5. The presence of the three Rosaries in the image of Our Lady of Guadalupe

The nucleus of all the mysteries of Salvation is the Cross, and by way of the Cross the mysteries of the three individual Rosaries penetrate each other. This co-penetration can be likened to the mystery of *perichorese* of the Most Holy TRINITY:[41] the FATHER is in the SON and the SON is in the FATHER and the HOLY SPIRIT preceeds from Both. In the One Person of CHRIST, and by His Cross as the sign of our redemption the three Rosaries are one, they become an image of the divine *perichorese*.

---

[41] This word is deep in sense: it also has to do with: "giving room, space to something" (Greek: chorein), cf. Mt. 19:11: in the sense: not everyone is able to take it. We have to make large, widen our heart. It is the LORD who reproaches the Pharisees that they do not open their heart for His Word - they do not give it the space necessary to unfold in them. St. Paul admonishes: *"do not lock yourself up, nobody suffered injustice from us."* (II COR 7:2) "Perichorein," the term used here, extends the sense to "mutual co-penetration." The Divine Persons give to Each Other plenty of space, to "feel at home with the Other." This is also the sense the LORD alludes to in His sermon of the Good Shepherd: *"Whoever enters through me will be safe, he will go in and out and find pasture"* (JN 10:9) The closer we come to GOD the more we will be allowed to have part in this Mystery of Perichorese, not only in view of the DIVINE PERSONS, but also in relation to each other!

We can see it, for example, in the co-penetration of the first mystery of each of the three Rosaries: Annunciation, Agony in the Garden and Resurrection.

The Annunciation to MARY is the first participation of Our Lady in the Agony of Our LORD. Man has never suffered a deeper solitude than has MARY after the Annunciation. Like the LORD in the Garden of Gethsemane, she had to carry the burden of this glory looking up only to GOD.

6. The significance of the "ring" or the "crown" of the Rosary in relation to the image of Our Lady of Guadalupe

The last fundament of the circling movement of our contemplation is the Life of the TRIUNE GOD, a Life which is exemplified by the RING OF LIGHT, symbol of GOD's eternal Beatitude. To this Destiny we are ordered as sons in the SON.

In the image of Guadalupe, the one "Ring of Light" of the various mysteries is visualized in the movement of the large flowers. They blossom forth from the Heart of the Mother of GOD, descend on her right side and ascend again on her left into the light. The movement is that of a spiral, as if on a vine, winding their way to the eternal light of GOD.

Just as all contemplation in the Holy Rosary encircles the one and triple central mystery of the Birth of CHRIST in our souls, so also does our contemplation of the image of Our Lady of Guadalupe encircle the final and victorious Birth of CHRIST in His Mystical Body and the whole of creation before it will return by and with the SON to the Heavenly FATHER.

B - IN RELATION TO THE INTERIOR HOUSE OF THE ROSARY (CF. II. 1. - 4.)

1. The Rosary as a house

a. The Presence of the Mysteries of Salvation in the image of Our Lady of Guadalupe.

In the image of Our Lady of Guadalupe, the mysteries of Salvation are like stones of construction. The mystery of opposition as the "motor" within the Rosary is reflected in the combat of light and darkness on Our Lady's earthen-toned gown. This opposition is also reflected in the multiple relations between the different symbols in the image, as well as in their orientation toward the mystery of the Birth of Our LORD signified in the four-petalled flower.

We enter the Movement of Ransom following the glance of Our Lady's loving eyes. Exactly at the point where the movement penetrates the deepest darkness the ascension begins.

This movement is another parable of the Incarnation, Crucifixion, Burial, Resurrection and Ascension. We observe the same movement of ransom with the star constellations on her mantle. They come to a symbolic resolution in the Constellation of the Leo, invisibly corresponding with the four-petalled flower on Our Lady's womb.[42] The LION OF JUDAH will overcome and finally bring back the whole of creation to the FATHER![43]

b. MARY as Fundament of the Church

That MARY is the fundament of the Church can be seen symbolically in the four columns on the lower part of her robe.

As with a rhombus, these four columns seem to spring from one hidden point in the lower fold of her garment. This point seems to concur with the

---

[42] The stars on the mantle of Our Lady of Guadalupe are exactly the Constellations of the 12th of December of 1531. Cf. Las Estrellas de la Virgen de Guadalupe, Centro de Estudios Guadalupanos, A.C., Historica, Colleccion I, 1981

[43] For a more detailed information, see *The Seven Veils of Our Lady of Guadalupe*.

seam of "the book."[44] The Four Columns indicate that the Church began with MARY and St. John at the foot of the Cross.[45]

c. The Presence of the TRIUNE GOD in this House
    The four-petalled flower is JESUS in the womb of His Virgin Mother. Looking closer at this flower we note a circle as its center. It is a detail that exem-

---

[44] The Four Gospels, the three Synoptics and the Gospel of St. John, signified in the booklike fold of her robe, represent the mystery of the Crucified LORD, Who finally will cover with the Cross the whole creation to bring it back to His FATHER.(cf.APOC 6:1-8: The Four Living Beings have this mission to extend the Cross over the whole world.) These Four Gospels are one in MARY who has received the wholeness of Salvation, so she really is the Fullness of the Gospel GOD is presenting us in these last times. In, by and with MARY Redemption will come to its final consummation. As the image of Our Lady of Guadalupe is the only authentic picture of Our Lady painted by the Hand of GOD Himself, it can be considered as the Fifth Gospel, not written by words, but by light. We will be able to read it only with the help of the Holy Angels, who being light, after Our Lady are closest to the LIGHT of GOD.

[45] The "boy" at Our Lady's feet, with the wings of "testimony," is her messenger. In beloved Apostle, St. John, he represents the purity of the priesthood - which at the end of times, crucified with the LORD, will announce the Fullness of the Gospel in, through and with MARY. St. Louis Marie de Montfort tells us the same about the apostles of the last times (also in his "fire prayer"!). The person of P. Pio of Pietrelcina, the first priest with the stigmata of the LORD, is a living gospel for the truth that these priests must be one with CHRIST CRUCIFIED!

plifies the presence of the TRIUNE GOD by way of the Incarnation. Within the Four Columns, the mystery of the Holy TRINITY will grow in CHRIST to its fullness.[46]

d. The Triple Birth of CHRIST in the Soul, in the central mysteries of the Rosary, are also symbolized in the circle in the center of the four-petalled flower.

2. The Indwelling of the TRIUNE GOD - His Birth in the Soul

a. A Birth in Glory

According to the glorious perspective of the image of Guadalupe, CHRIST's Birth in glory is emphasized. The Light of GOD pierces the darkness on the right side of her gown and pushes out all darkness from the left side.(A five-pointed star is seen falling in the ninth large flower: symbol of the fall of Lucifer.)[47]

---

[46] cf. EPH 4:13 and LK 2:40. This is also announced by the beatified Carmelite, Blessed Elizabeth of Most HOLY TRINITY. The Saints are the Living Gospel.

[47] The five-pointed star symbolizes the demonic captivity that encircles man's five extremities: his head, his outstretched arms and extended legs. In this dominant position we can see man's self-sufficiency imitating the revolt of Lucifer not wanting to submit to GOD's plans of wisdom concerning man. Only the Cross of Christ and His Five Wounds can break this captivity.

b. The 3 X 3 circles of the Rosary in the image of Guadalupe are represented by the nine large flowers. They are an image of our birth in CHRIST in nine steps, one which will lead into the light of transfiguration.

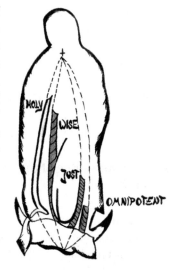

c. The "motor" of the Rosary is visualized in the image of Guadalupe by the Movement of Ransom. It is a movement that initiates in the Heart of GOD,[48] and becomes visible in the glance of the Virgin's eyes and the three fishing instruments: the light, the hook and the net with which she will bring home the last harvest.[49]

---

[48] The Heart of GOD is imaged in the Immaculate Heart of Our Lady; seen as a shadow on the outside of her left hand.

[49] The piercing light can be seen in the first Column representing the HOLY GOD; the fishing hook in the dark "U" formed by the following two Columns, the WISE and the JUST GOD; the fishing net can be seen in the fold of her mantle of the left arm which also can be interpreted as the mouth of a trumpet.

All opposition in the image is finally resolved in the four-petalled flower: the FATHER will bring home creation in the HOLY SPIRIT through the Cross of His SON by the mediation of MARY.

3. The Unfolding of the Life of JESUS in our Souls by action of the HOLY SPIRIT

The image of Our Lady of Guadalupe is, as are the icons of the Eastern Church, a guarantee of the presence of the Mother of GOD.[50] The fact that no two copies of this divine masterpiece is the same is another testimony of Our Lady's living presence. She always directs herself in a very personal way to anyone who will look up to her.

---

[50] By way of the golden quadrangle, it has been recently proven that every detail of the image is in absolute harmony with the whole. This also is one of the most convincing proofs that nothing has ever been added by human hand. This is why the image of Guadalupe is the most perfect among all the icons of the Mother of GOD. Over and above all the icons painted according to strict laws, the image of Our Lady of Guadalupe remains the best representation of the order of the Reign of GOD.

The more deeply we look up to contemplate her in her image of Guadalupe, the more the HOLY SPIRIT will impress her image in our souls, and by way of her, that of her SON.[51] Her SON is THE IMAGE OF THE INVISIBLE GOD.[52]

The crystalline purity of heart of Juan Diego enabled him to receive the image of the Virgin on behalf of all his country-men called to eternal life. Juan Diego is but an image of heaven's will to "Pinta," a la "Nina," la "Santa MARIA"[53] in the heart and soul of anyone who, like him, will consecrate his whole life to her.[54]

By way of her image, the Virgin Mother of Guadalupe really wants to accompany us wherever we go, so that by way of her the SON of GOD will take form in us. This is the deepest promise of this most perfect icon of Our Lady.

---

[51] The Nican Mopohua tells us in verse 27, *"En donde lo mostrare, lo ensalzare, al ponerlo de manifiesto;."* These words of the Virgin tell us of her utmost desire to "show us GOD" and to "give birth to Him." This "to give birth to Him" comes from the nahuatl meaning for the Spanish "ensalzar."

[52] cf. COL 1:15

[53] The names of the three ships of Columbus in the discovery of the New World really capture the interior message of Guadalupe as GOD's will to "paint" the "child" "Mary" in our souls so as to engender the SON in the HOLY SPIRIT.

[54] Nothing will help more than the consecration to Our Lady according to St. Louis M. de Montfort.

THE TRIUNE GOD WANTS TO
TAKE US HOME BY WAY
OF THE MOTHER OF HIS SON

The more we pray the Rosary contemplating her image, the more she herself will pray the mysteries of Salvation in us. The image of Guadalupe and the Rosary must help us to enter deeper in the movement of the Life of the TRIUNE GOD.

IV

DIFFERENT WAYS TO PRAY THE ROSARY[55]

A – LOOKING UP TO THE TRIUNE GOD

We have already pointed out the Trinitarian relation in the Rosary, so it is not necessary to explain why the Rosary should also be prayed in a "triune way."

1. Looking up to the FATHER:

We try to meditate the mysteries of Salvation in the Rosary as the way of the SON to the FATHER. We are invited with and through Him and with the help of Our Lady to join Him in this way to the FATHER.

Praying the Rosary this way in relation to the FATHER we participate in the dynamism of the movement of the SON towards the FATHER.

---

[55] These different ways to pray the Rosary do not imply that we have to pray them in a different way from the traditional. They are, first of all, different ways to enter into the mysteries of the Rosary, different perspectives to look on them, and a different way to make them incarnate in our life.

2. Looking up to the SON:

We should first of all concentrate on the mystery of His birth in us in the central mysteries, so that all the other mysteries should be seen in relation to this central mystery.

Concentrating on the SON, we try to put order in our lives by orientating all our interests on His Birth in our souls.

3. Looking up to the HOLY SPIRIT:

We try to find a very personal entry into the mysteries of the Rosary in order to become one with the mystery, which in a certain way is related to our existential situation.

In our looking up to the HOLY SPIRIT, we try to be more conscious of our special and unique vocation in the Mystical Body in the Church.

B – IN VIEW OF THE FOUR ESSENTIAL QUALITIES OF GOD[56]

The House of GOD in our soul must be fundamented on the Cross, but it should be seen in a triple way in

---

[56] Related to the Columns which constitute the Interior House of the Rosary

relation to the Three Holy Persons of the Most Holy TRINITY.

1. In the Joyful Mysteries, the house to be built in our souls is that of Nazareth where our life with GOD should be hidden before the eyes of the world.

2. In the Sorrowful Mysteries, the house should be the "Tower of David" which withstands all the attacks of the world and the devil, because in this house, the mystery of CHRIST the KING is growing.

3. By way of the Glorious Mysteries, the HOLY SPIRIT wants to build the house of glory in us, which already here on earth participates in the "mansions" the SON has prepared for us with the FATHER.[57]

   When we pray the Rosary in view of the Cross, we first of all ask for the protection of the Life of GOD mysteriously growing in us; here Our Lady is for us the "Tower of Ivory" (Joyful Mysteries), the "Tower of David" (Sorrowful Mysteries) and the "Strong Woman" (Glorious Mysteries).

---

[57] cf. JN 14:3

C – IN VIEW OF THE SEVEN GIFTS OF THE HOLY SPIRIT

The HOLY SPIRIT unfolds the Life of GOD in a seven-fold rhythm in us. If we want to pray the Rosary this way, we have to look back on the three circles of each Rosary, but we should reserve the three central mysteries, because in this perspective they will come at the end of the Rosary, united in one. The central mysteries are like the goal we are heading for.[58]

In view of the image of Our Lady of Guadalupe we propose another Rosary, "the Rosary of the Seven Veils," which will be presented in the Appendix. In this Rosary, the Birth of JESUS CHRIST in our souls is veiled as is the Birth of CHRIST in Our Lady, symbolically indicated by the four-petalled flower.

D – IN VIEW OF THE NINE STEPS OF THE BIRTH OF CHRIST IN OUR SOULS

Here the fifteen mysteries correspond to nine mysteries (3 x 3 circles) which we can relate to the nine choirs of the angels helping us in our birth into heaven.

---

[58] cf. II. 3. b. In this way we contract the Five Mysteries of each Rosary to two, corresponding to the two exterior circles and the three central mysteries are contracted to one.

Here, we should first of all be guided by the nine large flowers on the gown of Our Lady in their Movement of Ransom.

E – IN VIEW OF THE CONSUMMATION OF ALL THINGS IN THE NEW JERUSALEM

Here we pray the Rosary in view of the Four Qualities of GOD, but comprising the Three Rosaries as one.

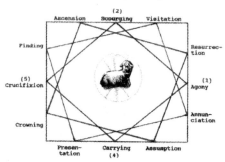

The twelve steps corresponding to the 3 X 4 mysteries of the two exterior circles should be related to the Twelve Gates of the New Jerusalem through which, one day, those who are called to eternal life will enter.

Once the Church has passed through all the mysteries of the Rosary, incarnating them to the fullness, the mystery of Salvation will have come to its end, and the New Jerusalem will be the precious fruit of the Cross for all eternity.

THE EUCHARISTIC CENTER
OF THE HOLY ROSARY

The foregoing meditations propose the question: **How can the triple Birth of Our LORD be seen as "one"?** How does the triple Birth of the LORD in our souls,[59] refer to Our LORD's Sacramental Presence in the Holy Eucharist?

Vatican Council II, by the inspiration of the HOLY SPIRIT, encourages our recognition of the living presence of the LORD present in our neighbor, especially when we come together as a sacred assembly; the LORD is in the midst of His people. But the presence of GOD, in and through our brothers, should never outshine the greater Sacramental Presence of CHRIST. Unfortunately, there is confusion concerning the abiding presence of the LORD in the Holy Sacrament of the Altar. Many of the faithful are led to believe that the tabernacle has no correspondence with the "liturgical space" of worship, and then there are so many who are not even aware of the dislocation of the tabernacle. **He who prays seeks the Face of the LORD**

Those who really seek the Face of the LORD are aware of this painful evolution. The whole-hearted longing for an ever deeper and personal encounter with HIM is what convinces the seeker of there being no other place where an encounter with the LIVING GOD is

---

[59]   It is a birth in joy, in sorrow and in glory.

most promising than before His Eucharistic Presence in the tabernacle.

Normally, our prayer is always in union with our angel. Although he continues in the beatific vision of GOD in heaven, he is most perfectly, with his entire being, orientated to the Eucharistic Presence of Our LORD. Certainly, the angelic knowledge of the Eucharistic Presence of JESUS CHRIST, and the poverty in which man responds to such a great grace, is what impulses the angels to make the Eucharistic LORD evermore loved and adored in these times of confusion.[60]

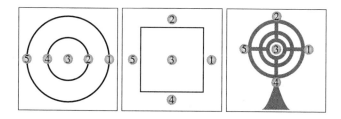

Guided by the HOLY SPIRIT in and throughout the evolution of the centuries, the Church opted for the consecration of unleavened round white hosts for that of

---

[60] Recall the angel's visits to the three shepherd children at Fatima to glimpse the angelic perspective with respect to the Holy Eucharist.

normal bread.[61] Not only does this action help distin-
guish the Eucharist from common bread, but it ties us
deeper with our Judeo roots of the Pesach tradition. The
round form of the host is a sign of perfection, **a sign of
the Circle of Light of the TRIUNE GOD.**

This is why we are allowed to relate the interior
circle of the Rosary, in comparison with the two circles
which surround it, in closer relation with the mystery of
the Holy Eucharist - as in another form it is indicated in
the image of Our Lady of Guadalupe in the rounded
four-petalled flower over her womb.

The Presence of Our LORD in the image of Our
Lady of Guadalupe, is not that of the historical JESUS,
but as we can see in the first chapter of the Gospel of
St. John, that of the Eucharistic LORD in the symbol
of the LAMB OF GOD. This relation is certainly something which should be much more emphasized in relation to the veneration given to the image of Our Lady
of Guadalupe. She not only wants to bring us closer to

---

61 The Eastern Church maintains the use of common bread for
consecration of the Holy Eucharist. In a liturgical preparation
before Holy Mass, the priest cuts this bread into little cubes
which will be consecrated to the Body of CHRIST. As was a
custom in the primitive church, the Eastern Church still blesses
the daily bread, and at the end of Mass, the faithful are allowed to take it home. The New Catechumenal Movement has
gone back to this tradition, apparently without contradiction
on the part of the hierarchical Church. Normally they celebrate
the Eucharist this way only in the close circle of those who
have been prepared and examined for a longer time.

her SON by her words and by her image, but she wants to turn our attention more and more to the Real Presence of Our LORD in the Holy Eucharist.[62]

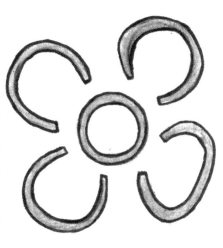

If we wish to pray the Rosary in the right way, we should not only look up to Our Lady in the image of Guadalupe, but first of all we should fix

---

[62] Here again we see how close this apparition of Our Lady of Guadalupe and her image are to the Gospel of St. John, who already in the first chapter, by way of St. John the Baptist, in the presence of the first Apostles, points to "THE LAMB OF GOD." Is not Our Lady of Guadalupe, in this apparition, and in all those which follow, another John the Baptist announcing the Second Coming of her SON which we have necessarily to see in relation with His Eucharistic Presence? The LORD will return in the same humble and hidden way, even more hidden as when HE came the first time. The Eucharist really, so much put aside in our times, is precisely the way where He enters into this world for the final separation of light and darkness. (cf. also Nican Mopohua, vs. 26-28, to note how Our Lady presents herself as a monstrance on behalf of the ONE and ONLY TRUE GOD)

our gaze on the four-petalled flower in which the Eucharistic Presence of Our LORD is alluded.

If we pray the Rosary in this Eucharistic dimension it will be lifted from the para-liturgical level of devotion to heart and center of all liturgy, the Holy Eucharist.[63]

The Triple Presence of Our LORD in the Most Holy Sacrament of the Altar

The Presence of the LORD in the Sacrament of the Holy Eucharist is not to be seen in a purely static way: "HE is simply there." We so easily get accustomed to His "mute

---

[63] "Praying the Rosary in the right way" means that we should respect the deeper relations of this prayer to the fundaments of our faith, and this not only in a material, but also in a formal way. Any "active participation" in liturgy, as proposed by the Vatican Council II always requires a certain preparation. We have to learn something about liturgical prayer, especially about its form and its mode before we can fully participate (with profit for ourselves and for those who also participate in it). This also holds true as we previously tried to expose for the prayer of the Rosary in which we really encounter something of the Holy Order of the Reign of GOD. In this perspective, the pious way of participating in the Latin Mass before the Vatican Council II certainly was not so much out of order as it is considered in a purely exterior consideration of the liturgy. It certainly helped those who prayed it with their heart to approach the LORD more than any exterior participation which sometimes helps to hide our interior distraction.

presence" that we forget that He is **really** there. The Holy Eucharist must be seen in the dynamic sense: calling out in the HOLY SPIRIT, bringing in those who are afar, convincing us in our hearts.[64] Lastly, His Presence in the tabernacle and also in Holy Mass should be seen in the HOLY SPIRIT as "a field of influence" in which those who pray feel at home and receive force for their daily Christian combat.

As litttle Therese, we should learn to carry Our LORD from one Communion to the next, and thus become a living tabernacle, making thc Church present wherever we carry the LORD. This is only possible if we wrap the Eucharistic LORD up, as did MARY, in our permanent prayer and contemplation. He should feel at home with and in us, as in MARY or as at Bethany, so as to irradiate to the world His Light of Salvation. Here certainly the Rosary could be a great help because it will help us to be always orientated to the one center:

---

[64] This dynamic Presence of the LORD is not limited to the Holy Mass in which the LORD comes to us by way of the Sacrifice of Golgatha. Before the Vatican Council II the dynamic Presence of Our LORD during Holy Mass was hardly emphasized. Now that the tides have turned, it has been placed in the forelight to the point of forgetting about Our LORD's static permanence in the Blessed Sacrament of the Altar. This is one of the reasons why the sacramental presence of Our LORD in the tabernacle has been pushed aside. Both of the other components: His dynamic Presence and His "field of influence" are also present in His Eucharistic permanence in the tabernacle.

the LORD. If we pray the Rosary with our angel, he will turn our thinking, speaking and doing continually to this Presence of Our LORD in us so that we can always be in prayer.

Through the Rosary, the maternal love of MARY wants to make a bridge over the gap of popular piety and theological erodition.[65] Just as the Virgin of Guadalupe told Juan Diego to cut and gather the roses atop Tepeyac to be "the sign" for Bishop Zumarraga, so also now do we do knock with the Holy Rosary at the door of Holy Mother Church.

Dedicated to St. Michael
On the former Feast of his apparition in Monte
Gargano
Fatima 5-8-94
m.g.

---

[65] This gap has broadened ever since the late Medieval Age and has opened the door to heresies on both sides. On the one hand there is the danger of a piety foreign to the official liturgy of the Church, on the other-hand rationalistic ideologies foment and contaminate the theology of the Church.

THE SEVEN VEILS
OF OUR LADY OF
GUADALUPE

1. Clouds
2. Rays
3. Mantle
4. Gown
5. Inner Gown
6. Body
7. Soul

The Seven Veils of Our Lady of Guadalupe help us to recognize MARY as the "Ark of the New Covenant," veiled with seven veils. They form part of the "Holy Rhythm of Seven"[66] and act as a "lighted spiral" opening our souls to the Greater Beauty of GOD, not only in the image, but in the person of Our Lady of Guadalupe

---

[66] The "Rhythm of Seven" is a rhythm of divine origin revealed at the creation of the world. We recognize something of it in all the "groups of seven," i.e. the Seven Days of Creation, the seven Liturgical Hours, the Seven Sacraments, the Seven Gifts of the HOLY SPIRIT, Our LORD's Seven Last Words from the Cross, the Seven Communities of Asia, the seven divisions of Holy Mass, the Seven Archangels, etc.

who is the Monstrance who *"bears, reveals, extols and manifests"* the Mystery of GOD.[67]

The Seven Veils of the *"Ever Perfect Virgin Mother"* can be likened to seven steps leading to an encounter with *"the True GOD, the Creator of all Persons, the LORD of Salvation History, the LORD of Heaven and Earth."*[68] They help us on our own "spiritual pilgrimage" to her "house" where she wants to reveal GOD to us in all His Glory.[69] Going to her house is at the same time: "building her a house in our hearts," where more and more the HOLY SPIRIT will transform us into the image of her SON.

---

[67]   Cf. Nican Mopohua, vs. 27

[68]   These are the translations of the nahuatl (aztec) terms Our Lady used in her first apparition to Juan Diego.(cf. Nican Mopohua, vs.26).

[69]   cf. Nican Mopohua, vs.27

Each Veil is prayed, contemplating her image "in the spirit," such that she can also look down upon us and take us into her merciful eyes.[70] The more she looks on us, the more we will be transformed in her, becoming "another Mary," so that when GOD looks down on us through her, HE will first of all find the Mother of His Most Beloved SON. This should happen more and more with each of us who follow the LORD on His way up to Golgatha, so that "the little flock" will be transformed into MARY Immaculate, standing at the foot of the Cross.

The grace of entering into any of the "Veils" should always be made on behalf of all those entrusted to our care so that they also may partake in the merciful assistance of Our Lady's mantle. In a very unique way, in union with Our Blessed Mother and the Holy Angels, we can join in all the other "groups" of seven as a means of sanctifying each hour of everyday as well as everyday of the week.[71] The contemplation of the Veils be-

---

[70] Macro-photography and digitized computer amplification have found a family of 12 persons in the eyes of the Virgin of Guadalupe.

[71] We only need to relate each veil to the corresponding veil or day of the week. In this way we are ever more "under the mantle of Our Lady," and this always in a different and significative way which will help us to more deeply understand the symbolical value of the veils. In the confusion and anarchy of today's age, this will help us to live more and more consciouly the order of the Reign of GOD. It is even a way of healing the bad consequences of modern civilization: stress, restlessness, disharmony!

comes a disposition for a fuller reception of the Seven Gifts of the HOLY SPIRIT.

Our entry into this "rhythm of grace," by way of the Veils of the Virgin, is an entry into the source of all grace, the Eucharistic Heart of Our LORD JESUS CHRIST. Wherever Our LORD is, there also we find Our Lady and the Holy Angels. They pass His call of love on to everyone of us, reminding us throughout the day that everything we think, speak or do is first of all orientated to HIM and to His Greater Glory. Only in this way our works and deeds can one day be found worthy of entering heaven.

ONE WAY OF PRAYING THE SEVEN VEILS

A. Begin with the Sign of the Cross. We adore GOD's Eternal Wisdom in chosing it as the instrument of our salvation, we confess the Holy Cross as the symbol of our faith and we beseech to be sealed by and in it. We remember that to be sealed with the Holy Cross is a unique privilege which not only brings special graces, but great responsibilities.

B. Nine times we pray the Sanctus; one time for and with each of the heavenly choirs. We begin with our own Guardian Angel, and all guardian angels, and continue by invoking the Archangels, Virtues, Principalities, Powers, Dominations, Thrones, Cherubim and Seraphim. Praying in union with the entire Heavenly Court has great value and significance. The Holy Angels are always before GOD, adoring and glorifying Him. It is they who carry our prayers to the Heart of the Holy, Mighty and Immortal GOD.

A Schematic View:

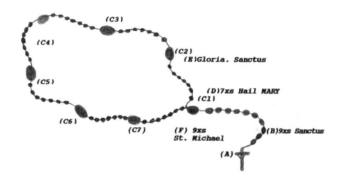

(A) The Sign of the Cross
(B) 9xs Holy, Holy, Holy
(C) Our Father (The Particular Veil)
(D) 7xs Hail MARY (meditating the correlations)
(E) After each Veil, pray the Gloria and the Holy, Holy (continue with each corresponding veil, C.2, C.3,....etc.)
(F) St. Michael Prayer 9xs

C.1 The First Veil: **THE CLOUDS**; already, the first veil will take us into the contemplation of the mystery of GOD, symbolized in the cloud, ie. MARY (cf. IKings 19:12b), the mysterious presence of GOD (cf. Ex 13:21, Nm 9:15, I Rom 8:10), another attribute of the "One and Only True GOD," Ometéotl, "He that covers the earth with cotton."[72] The first veil, representing the mystery of GOD, is the foundation of the participation in the Life of GOD.

Liturgical Hour: **Matins**; the first "hour" given to us by GOD. We unite ourselves with the light of the new day and we begin the day with hearts filled with praise and adoration of GOD, the Author and Origin of "The Light."

Sacrament: **The Most Holy Eucharist**; we recognize in the first lights of the day, as in the clouds, the first opportunity for making a spiritual communion and for receiving "the Mysterious One." It also gives us our sacramental orientation: The BREAD of LIFE at the beginning of the new day.

Gift of the HOLY SPIRIT: **Understanding**; the light of understanding which we are lacking is received from Our LORD JESUS CHRIST truly present in the Most Holy Eucharist. Adoration of Our LORD in this Sacrament of Love and Light is the goal of the Holy Angels

---

[72] This is a poetic expression used by the wise man (tlamantini) of the Aztecs.

with respect to mankind. It is their only desire to bring all creation to the Heart of GOD.

C.2 The Second Veil: **The Rays**; fire, light, energy and radiation emanating from the Most Holy Virgin, demonstrating that she herself bears the fountain and source of all life. The sun, for the Aztecs, was one of the most important symbols of GOD as the source and origin of all that is, "The GOD from Whom we have our existence," *IN IPALNEMOHUANI*. When we speak of the Love of GOD, we speak of a reality that all purified souls experience. It is the Divine Love which consumes. We see, in MARY, a fire which is now the soul of her being, of her Immaculate Heart. It is a mystical marriage between her, the "Immaculate Conception" and her Spouse: GOD. *"With you is Wisdom who knows your works, who was with you when you made the world, who knows what is favorable in your sight,..."* Wisdom 9:9.

Liturgical Hour:: **Lauds**; the morning prayer which prepares us for the Sacrifice of Holy Mass, the living expression of the saving Love of GOD. Through the Light of GOD which has already reached us, we are able to recognize not only the beauties of nature, but the wonders of the Redemptive Work of Our LORD JESUS CHRIST and this is why "the colors" are radiant with praise, reflecting the Author and source of all life.

Sacrament: **Matrimony**; the Sacrament of Life of the propagation of the family of GOD. The 138 visible rays (1+3+8=12) in the Image of Our Lady of Guadalupe teach us of the finality of the family: the Consummation of the Love of GOD in the New Jerusalem.

Gift of the HOLY SPIRIT: **Wisdom**; teaching us that GOD is Author, Origin, Creator and Omega. All the names and attributes given by the Blessed Virgin in the first apparition (Dec. 9, 1531 demonstrate this holy Wisdom of GOD. (cf. Nican Mopohua vs 26; **In Huelnelli Téotl Dios**: GOD of Great Truth, **In Ipalnemohuani**: He from Whom all being has existence, **In Teoyocoyani**: Creator of mankind (of Self and of others), **In Tloque Nahuaque**: The LORD of all that surrounds and touches our lives. It is also translated to "He Whom supersedes us," this is the name of the GOD of history. **In Ilhuicahua in Tlaltipaque**: The LORD of the heaven and earth, **Teimattini**: The Provider. Another sign of the union of GOD and the Holy Virgin is found in the Book of Wisdom 9:9, "With you is Wisdom who knows your works, who was with you when you made the world, who knows what is favorable in your sight,..."

C.3 The Third Veil: **Her Mantle**; symbol of protection, of water, of the sea, of life, of the heavens, of the angels and of "xihuitl" (all that is precious in the heavens and on earth). The gospel of the stars found with the constellations represented on her mantle announce in and through the light. Here, we can make a beautiful tie with the Annunciation of the Archangel Gabriel. He, as the Guardian of the earth, proclaims the Good News to

MARY. He brings the Word of GOD to her and she responds to His voice with her *"Fiat Mihi, secundum Verbum Tuum."* This reminds us also of the third day of Creation; by her fiat, this earth became firm.

Liturgical Hour: **Terce**; the hour which is our entrance into the work of the day. We go forth from Holy Mass, carrying the Word of GOD to the world; this is mission. As the seer, Juan Diego, represented in the child at the feet of the Virgin holds tightly onto the mantle of his Mother, let us enter into this hour under the mantle of her protection.

Sacrament: **Baptism**; the Sacrament of New Life which incorporates us into the family of GOD, giving us dignity and an eternal mission.

Gift of the HOLY SPIRIT: **Counsel**; the Gift that orients us to GOD. The Holy Angels, symbolized in the stars of the mantle of the Virgin of Tepeyac, are light and orientation on our way and journey to GOD. The counsel and advice to all Christians is to live one's Baptism so that with, through and in MARY we are enabled to be "servants and handmaids of the LORD."

C.4 The Fourth Veil: **Her Tunic**; is of an earthly-toned color and in a certain sense reflects salvation history in its entirety. We recognize in the play of lights and darkness a teaching on the Cross and the spiritual battle in which we must participate if we wish to live united with the Master. We note that a lace of golden flowers is superimposed on her tunic. This speaks to us of the heavenly assistance of the Holy Angels in our daily battles. It also tells us of their desire to participate in the Passion of Our LORD JESUS CHRIST. The four-petalled flower, the "nahui ollín," is cruciform and speaks to us of sacrificial life in GOD, also the other nine small eight-petalled flowers: we need to be crucified with CHRIST in order to live our common priesthood.

Liturgical Hour: **Sext**; midday, being the hour in which Our LORD was raised up on the Cross, it should be for us the hour of transformation. Let us unite ourselves with this liturgical hour that we also may benefit from the graces of His Sacred Passion. It is an hour in which we can reflect, examining and seeing our lives in the light of the Holy Cross, participating in the Redemptive Work of CHRIST.

Sacrament: **Penance**; the Sacrament of purification. By the grace of the Sacred Passion and the Most Precious Blood of Our LORD JESUS CHRIST we can experience the healing and transforming waters of this Sacrament. We ask for the grace of preparing ourselves well so as to benefit from the fullness of the Sacrament of Penance.

Gift of the HOLY SPIRIT: **Knowledge** (of the Cross); This Gift isn't learned from books or studying. It is the science taught by GOD Himself in the Sacrifice of His Only SON. Like MARY, we should participate in the Redemptive Work of Her SON.

C.5 The Fifth Veil: **HER INTERIOR WHITE TUNIC**; white is the color reflecting her angelic purity, symbol of the peaks of the Mexican volcanoes Popocatépetl and Iztaccihuatl, covered by snow year round.

Liturgical Hour: **None**; the hour of the Death of Our LORD JESUS CHRIST. His total surrender to the will of His FATHER is the surrender that fortifies us in this vale of tears. It is a time of thanksgiving, of repentance and of resolution. It is a time for the saving graces of the SON of GOD.

Sacrament: **Holy Orders**; We pray for all priests, especially those in most need of the Mercy of GOD. We beseech the grace of MARY's angelic purity for all priests such that they may be fortified in her purity.

Gift of the HOLY SPIRIT: **Fortitude**; the most necessary Gift in these times of battle against the impurities of the world. Let us ask for the Fortitude of the HOLY SPIRIT through the purity of MARY. MARY's purity is really a total surrender as the "Spouse of GOD." We pray that our surrender, fortified in the purity of MARY, be a strength for the entire Church...that we may be a worthy response to the will of Our LORD JESUS CHRIST in his command, *"love one another as I have loved you."* (JN 13:34)

C.6 Sixth Veil: **HER BODY**; only her hands and her face are seen. In her left hand we see the shadow of Her

Immaculate Heart, and in her glance we encounter but a shadow of the infinite and Merciful Love of GOD.

Liturgical Hour: **Vespers;** it is the hour when we come to the end of the day's work and once again we present it to the LORD. It is also the hour in which we unite ourselves with the Archangel of the Love of GOD, St. Raphael, and ask for his powerful and special assistance. Vespers brings to mind the mercy and compassion exercised by the holy women after the lifeless body of Our LORD was taken down from the Cross. If we pray this hour with St. Raphael, we can beseech him to wound us with his arrow of love, that we are never healed from this wound.....and that all is conquered through love.

Sacrament: **Confirmation**; it is the Sacrament in which we promise to live a Christian life. As it is the Sacrament of the HOLY SPIRIT, let us ask for all His Gifts, but most especially for the Fear of the LORD. The Virginal Body and Soul of Our Blessed Mother received the HOLY SPIRIT and the power of the Most High overshadowed her (cf. LK 1:35) making of her "the promised woman" of Genesis 3:15. It is she who will "crush the head of the serpent." It is through her that we are enabled to live our Confirmation and we announce her, with all the heavenly court, "Conqueror of hell"!

Gift of the HOLY SPIRIT: **Fear of the LORD**; this Gift teaches us Wisdom. It is the just distance between the Creator and the creature. The Gift is recognized in both the Virgin's hands and face, namely that part of her virginal body that shows: her hands, in the praying position, and her inclined head, both gestures of profound reverence of GOD, her Creator.

C.7 Seventh Veil: **HER SOUL**; Our Lady's soul cannot be seen, but as a veil of the mystery of GOD Whom she bears, it is present in her glance and in the "movement of ransom" which comes forth from the same. Thru her merciful eyes, we recognize her to be the great fishermaid. With the Holy Angels, she prepares the great harvest.

Liturgical Hour: **Complines**; it is the hour when we commend our spirits unto the LORD. Night Prayer offers us the grace to remember that one day the hour of our own death will approach, so we ask for the preparatory grace of final repentance.

Sacrament: **Anointing of the Sick**; the Sacrament which prepares us for our encounter and judgement with and by GOD. It is here, at this hour that we beseech the particular intercession of the Prince of the Heavenly Hosts, St. Michael the Archangel, in the preparation of our final hour, but we should not limit our prayer of his assistance to this final hour; for his help is a continual aid...."*for you do not know the day of your Master's return.*" (Mt 24:42) St. Michael is the great patron of the Holy Mother, the Church, and it is his mission to help us in our daily battles and in our last journey, it is he who is to carry us to the other shore!

The Gift of the HOLY SPIRIT: **Piety**; the seventh Gift of the HOLY SPIRIT. GOD wills to encounter the Heart and Soul of MARY Immaculate in every member of the Mystical Body of His SON so as to fully live His incarnate mystery of Love in all. We must ask for the grace to be a child of MARY, living the "Who is Like unto GOD" of St. Michael such that we live and give a worship worthy of God's majesty.[73]

---

[73] This formal presentation of the Seven Veils is not meant as a restriction to the mode or manner in which it can be prayed. It is presented as a "help" for praying any of the groupings of seven. It can be prayed formally at any given time or as a silent reflection corresponding to the liturgical hour of the day.

Scheme for Meditation
in the "rhythm of seven"

Clouds	Matins	Holy Eucharist	Understanding	Ephesus	"Father, forgive them for they know not what they do."	Introit
Rays	Lauds	Marriage	Wisdom	Smyrna	"This day you will be with me in paradise."	Readings
Mantle	Terce	Baptism	Counsel	Pergamum	"Behold your Mother."	Offertory
Gown	Sext	Penance	Science	Thyatira	"I thirst."	Sanctus
Inner Gown	None	Holy Orders	Fortitude	Sardis	"My GOD, my GOD, why have You abandoned me?"	Consecration
Body	Vespers	Confirmation	Fear of the Lord	Philadelphia	"It is consummated."	Communion
Soul	Complines	Extreme Unction	Piety	Laodicea	Complines	"Ita Missa est."

ABOUT THE AUTHOR

Anonymous writings were the rule in the Middle Ages, because what matters is the contents of books and not the person of the author. For the most part, works which bear the name of no man, imply the source of inspiration as being Divine, that is, crediting the work as having a sole author, namely, GOD, the Creator and Author of all that is: material and immaterial, including our very thoughts. Even before we begin to contemplate THE IMAGE OF OUR LADY OF GUADALUPE, we need to fundament ourselves in the reality that GOD alone is Author, Center and Finality.

More than a name, Miguel Guadalupe should be a concrete symbol of GOD's authorship. By way of the pseudonym, the book is characterized as a member of the family of Our Lady, specifically of Our Lady of Guadalupe; a title given to Our Lady, as well as her miraculous Image, by Holy Mother the Church shortly after her appearances to Juan Diego in Mexico, in 1531. As *"the woman clothed with the sun and the moon beneath her feet,"* she is the *"Great Sign"* who not only marks the brink of Modern Times, but who also by way of St. Michael wages war against the *"dragon."* (cf. Apoc. 12:1, 12:7)

Miguel is the Spanish name for Michael, the Archangel and "Prince of the Heavenly Hosts," for he also has his part in *The Seven Veils of Our Lady of Guadalupe*. It is in San Miguel del Milagro, Mexico, the only Church approbated apparition site of St. Michael in North America (apparitions of St. Michael 1631), and then in missions throughout Mexico, the U.S.A. and several European countries, that this topic was first treated. The book was written in team work and aims at creating "family" with the One Necessary Center, symbolized by the "nahui ollin," the four-petalled flower on the womb of Our Lady of Guadalupe. It is a hidden promise that she will bring Our LORD to this world again, veiled by the same seven veils which surround His Eucharistic Presence among us.

The Second Coming of Our LORD, even though at the end it will be like a lightning bolt, is necessarily linked to His Eucharistic Presence. For this we have to give testimony as the martyr St. Jeanne D'Arc, who daily received Holy Communion and listened to the voice of St. Michael the Archangel. Nobody knew about this element of her mission, but she was still burned at the stake as a heretic in 1431, exactly 100 years before the apparitions of Our Lady in 1531. Something similar might happen to the remnant of faithful souls who are ready to "wash their garments in the Blood of the LAMB." They are already being gathered by the "Hidden LORD" from the "four winds."

THE IMAGE OF OUR LADY OF GUADALUPE, with the assistance of St. Michael the Archangel, should be like unto the banner of St. Jeanne, leading to the victory and Triumph of the Immaculate Heart of MARY by way of St. Michael's cry "Who like unto GOD." The Image should penetrate the deepest part of our souls so that not only exteriorly we are assured of her living presence with us, but by way of her, become that "new man" we are called to be in CHRIST JESUS. It is thus that the threefold creation: material, angel and man, come together to sing the eternal praises of the TRIUNE GOD.

May 13, 1995